Matthias Stürmer

How Firms Make Friends: Communities in Private-Collective Innovation

Matthias Stürmer

How Firms Make Friends: Communities in Private-Collective Innovation

Building sources of sustained competitive advantage through contributing to open source projects

Südwestdeutscher Verlag für Hochschulschriften

Impressum/Imprint (nur für Deutschland/ only for Germany)
Bibliografische Information der Deutschen Nationalbibliothek: Die Deutsche Nationalbibliothek verzeichnet diese Publikation in der Deutschen Nationalbibliografie; detaillierte bibliografische Daten sind im Internet über http://dnb.d-nb.de abrufbar.

Alle in diesem Buch genannten Marken und Produktnamen unterliegen warenzeichen-, marken- oder patentrechtlichem Schutz bzw. sind Warenzeichen oder eingetragene Warenzeichen der jeweiligen Inhaber. Die Wiedergabe von Marken, Produktnamen, Gebrauchsnamen, Handelsnamen, Warenbezeichnungen u.s.w. in diesem Werk berechtigt auch ohne besondere Kennzeichnung nicht zu der Annahme, dass solche Namen im Sinne der Warenzeichen- und Markenschutzgesetzgebung als frei zu betrachten wären und daher von jedermann benutzt werden dürften.

Verlag: Südwestdeutscher Verlag für Hochschulschriften Aktiengesellschaft & Co. KG
Dudweiler Landstr. 99, 66123 Saarbrücken, Deutschland
Telefon +49 681 37 20 271-1, Telefax +49 681 37 20 271-0
Email: info@svh-verlag.de
Zugl.: Zürich, ETH, Dissertation, 2009

Herstellung in Deutschland:
Schaltungsdienst Lange o.H.G., Berlin
Books on Demand GmbH, Norderstedt
Reha GmbH, Saarbrücken
Amazon Distribution GmbH, Leipzig
ISBN: 978-3-8381-1379-1

Imprint (only for USA, GB)
Bibliographic information published by the Deutsche Nationalbibliothek: The Deutsche Nationalbibliothek lists this publication in the Deutsche Nationalbibliografie; detailed bibliographic data are available in the Internet at http://dnb.d-nb.de.

Any brand names and product names mentioned in this book are subject to trademark, brand or patent protection and are trademarks or registered trademarks of their respective holders. The use of brand names, product names, common names, trade names, product descriptions etc. even without a particular marking in this works is in no way to be construed to mean that such names may be regarded as unrestricted in respect of trademark and brand protection legislation and could thus be used by anyone.

Publisher: Südwestdeutscher Verlag für Hochschulschriften Aktiengesellschaft & Co. KG
Dudweiler Landstr. 99, 66123 Saarbrücken, Germany
Phone +49 681 37 20 271-1, Fax +49 681 37 20 271-0
Email: info@svh-verlag.de

Printed in the U.S.A.
Printed in the U.K. by (see last page)
ISBN: 978-3-8381-1379-1

Copyright © 2010 by the author and Südwestdeutscher Verlag für Hochschulschriften Aktiengesellschaft & Co. KG and licensors
All rights reserved. Saarbrücken 2010

How Firms Make Friends: Communities in Private-Collective Innovation

Matthias Stürmer

When firms contribute to open source projects, they in fact invest into public goods which may be used by everyone, even by their competitors. This seemingly paradoxical behavior is explained by the model of private-collective innovation where private investors participate in collective action. Previous literature explains that companies benefit through the production process providing them with unique incentives such as learning and reputation effects. By contributing to such open source projects firms are able to build a network of external individuals and organizations, who may participate in the creation and development of the software. As will be shown in this doctoral dissertation firm-sponsored communities involve the formation of interorganizational relationships which eventually may lead to a source of sustained competitive advantage. However, managing a largely independent open source community is a challenging balancing act between exertion of control to appropriate value creation, and openness in order to gain and preserve credibility and motivate external contributions.

Table of Content

1. The Balancing Act of Community Management..5
2. Communities of Open Source Projects..8
   2.1. Motivation..8
   2.2. Governance..9
   2.3. Competitive Dynamics...12
   2.4. Characterizing Firm-Sponsored Open Source Projects.........................14
   2.5. The Private-Collective Model of Innovation.................................16
3. Research Framework..18
   3.1. Filling Gaps in the Literature...18
   3.2. Extending the Open Innovation Paradigm.....................................19
   3.3. Nokia's Entrance Into the Open Source Industry.............................20
   3.4. Antecedents of Intrinsic and Extrinsic Motivation..........................21
4. Three Cases of Firm-Sponsored Open Source Communities.............................22
   4.1. Eclipse by IBM...22
   4.2. Maemo by Nokia...24
   4.3. Openmoko by Openmoko Inc...27
5. Conclusions and Implications..30
   5.1. The Concept of Interorganizational Competitive Advantage:
        Towards a Related Research Agenda..31
   5.2. Impact on Theory and Practice..40
   5.3. Future Research Agenda...42

References...46

1. The Balancing Act of Community Management

Creation and appropriation of value are the two core elements of every firm's business model. Therefore a company usually protects its assets in order to appropriate their value exclusively. Since knowledge represents one of the key sources of competitive advantage (Grant, 1996), there exist various ways for a firm to protect its intellectual property (Liebeskind, 1996). Surprisingly, empirical research on open source software has shown that in certain cases firms do not conceal their knowledge but actively reveal it publicly (Lerner and Tirole, 2002; Lee and Cole, 2003; Henkel, 2006). The behavior of investing in public goods for the purpose of increasing private profits has been coined as the private-collective model of innovation (von Hippel and von Krogh, 2003; 2006). Small as well as large software companies release previously proprietary software under open source licenses, they employ engineers who program code for publicly available open source software, and they sponsor the creation and maintenance of volunteer and partner firm communities. Obviously, making friends seems to be an attractive option for many firms to support their innovation activities.

It is known that community building is one of the major goals in all open source projects (Stuermer, 2005). However, if a profit-oriented organization intends to create an innovating community, this task becomes particularly challenging. On the one hand, volunteers may become suspicious if a firm invests in a public good because the main objective of a for-profit company is to maximize corporate profits (Bae and Cameron, 2006). On the other hand, while engineers within a company follow hierarchical control, communities outside the boundaries of the firm act independently based on their individual motivations (Dahlander and Wallin, 2006). Therefore, firms have to find other ways than direct control in order to induce contributions to their open source projects. Dahlander and Magnusson (2005) argue that firms should follows a symbiotic approach. By giving knowledge assets to the community and respecting its norms and values, firms are able to exert means of subtle control in their interaction with the community.

Nevertheless, successfully building and maintaining a thriving community remains a challenging task for a firm. Academic researchers as well as practitioners are thus interested to better understand the characteristics of corporate-sponsored open source communities and find the mechanisms how firms are able to facilitate the creation of such networks. Research so far has identified firm-driven communities as valuable assets for companies (Dahlander and Wallin, 2006; West and O'Mahony, 2008), but has omitted in-depth empirical analyses on why and how companies benefit from their communities. Therefore, this thesis takes up the concept of private-collective innovation, extends its perception of firm-driven communities, and suggests an integration with an existing model in the strategic management literature.

As has been explained, an active open source community of a firm is a resource difficult to imitate. Therefore once a company has reached the position of an influential participant within a community and can appropriate value from the community's innovations, it has gained so-called interorganizational competitive advantage. This concept by Dyer and Singh (1998) constitutes an alternative to the industry structure view by Porter (1980) and the resource-based view by Wernerfelt (1984) and Barney (1991) and is also called the 'relational view'. It explains why interfirm resources and routines embedded in a network of relationships represent a sustainable competitive advantage. As will be shown in the concluding section, firm-sponsored open source communities in private-collective innovation represent a perfect example of such interorganizational competitive advantage.

The present doctoral thesis consists of an opening chapter and three independent research papers in the references co-authored by the writer of this thesis. This opening chapter presents a literature overview on open source communities, the research framework of the three pivotal papers, a summary of three firm-sponsored projects, and a synthesis of the empirical findings positioned as example of the relational view. Each of the three dissertation papers in the references elaborates a different perspective on firm-sponsored open source projects. The first paper "Enabling Knowledge Creation through Outsiders: Towards a Push Model of Open Innovation" provides insight on open source development by IBM pointing out knowledge creation deficiencies in the current conception of open innovation. The second paper "Extending private-collective innovation: a case study" presents an in-depth qualitative analysis of a corporate sponsored open source project by Nokia explaining benefits and costs of this distributed type of innovation initiative. And the third paper "The credible sponsor: Participants' motivation and organization attributes in collaborative digital innovation" looks at the sponsoring effect on individual's motivation and on their performance.

2. Communities of Open Source Projects

Research on open source projects is attractive because of their impact on economy and society, the theoretical puzzles they pose, the availability of data, the reflexivity of their communities, and the parallels with science (von Krogh and Spaeth, 2007). The current literature on open source software research can be grouped into three different areas (von Krogh and von Hippel, 2006): Motivation, governance, and competitive dynamics. In the following, an overview of research in these three areas is presented with emphasis on firm-driven open source projects and their communities. Then, the concepts of community- and firm-driven projects will be contrasted followed by an introduction to the private-collective model of innovation.

2.1. Motivation

The first stream of literature on open source software treats the issue of motivation. Discovering the underlying cause for contributing to open source projects has been one of the most puzzling mysteries for social scientists. A single motivational factor has not been found. However, a thorough review of current research on open source projects shows that the motivation among participants is highly diverse. Von Krogh and colleagues (2009) found ten different incentives for participation in open source projects, namely ideology, altruism, kinship amity, enjoyment, reputation, reciprocity, learning, own-use value, career, and pay. These motives, categorized into intrinsic, internalized extrinsic, and extrinsic motivations, have been studied widely by a multitude of researchers (Lerner and Tirole, 2002; Hars and Ou, 2002; Lakhani and von Hippel, 2003; Hertel et al., 2003; Roberts et al., 2006; Steward and Gosain, 2006; Wu et al., 2007).

While programmers in the early days of open source development were mostly driven by intrinsic and internalized extrinsic motives, the importance of extrinsic incentives has increased in recent years (O'Mahony, 2007). One example is the development of Linux. When Linus Torvalds and colleagues started to program their operating system, they were mostly driven by fun and other intrinsic motives spending much of their spare time on their computer hobby (Raymond, 1999). Today, however, at least 73 percent of contributions come from employees of software corporations (Red Hat, Novell, IBM, Intel etc.) or the foundation itself, as reported by the Linux Foundation in a recent study (Kroah-Hartman et al., 2008). This shows that even in initially noncommercial open source projects the influence of firms may rise and new motivational structures can become important. When extrinsic incentives are introduced in intrinsically motivated communities, crowding-out effects may occur leading to an overall decrease of activity (Frey and Oberholzer-Gee, 1997; Frey and Jegen, 2001; Alexy and Leitner, 2008). And when software companies *start* an open source project themselves still other incentives are important to attract external contributions (Dahlander and Magnusson, 2005; von Krogh and von Hippel, 2006). One of the dissertation papers (Stuermer et al., 2009) treats the case where Nokia initiated an own-branded open source platform and built a community for it. Benefits and costs of this effort are analyzed and best practices of Nokia are elaborated.

2.2. Governance

The second area of open source research is devoted to governance. Governing organizational and production processes in open source projects is related to motivational issues, but involves also challenges of its own. Markus (2007) defines governance of open source projects as "the means of achieving the direction, control, and coordination of wholly or partially autonomous individuals and organizations on behalf of an OSS development project to which they jointly contribute." Governance of an open source project thus includes the management of a more or less independent community by a few individuals who are in charge of control. Markus (2007) states that governance in fact solves the motivational problem by empowering open source contributors and giving them control, ownership, and the opportunity to utilize the benefits of their investments. In this way governance of an open source project resolves the collective action dilemma by mechanisms such as open source licenses (Franck and Jungwirth, 2003; Lee and Cole, 2003; Henkel, 2006) and non-profit foundations (O'Mahony, 2003; O'Mahony and Bechky, 2008). Another perspective on overcoming the collective action problem is presented in the private-collective model of innovation which will be explained below (von Hippel and von Krogh, 2003).

Governance substantially differs between community-driven and firm-managed open source projects. In a community-initiated project, governance structures evolve bottom-up through a meritocratic process providing those authority who engaged in technical contributions and organizational-building behavior (O'Mahony and Ferraro, 2007). If a heterogeneous community controls an open source project, principles such as independence and decentralized decision-making prevail (O'Mahony, 2007). On the other hand, if firms found an open source project, its governance structure has to serve a different goal. Since firms can exist in the long run only if they are profitable, appropriation regimes are required to capture the profits generated by innovations (Teece, 1986). Therefore, companies which invest into the creation of open source code must somehow govern their project in a way that allows them to capture the created value. This suggests that firms need control of critical aspects of the innovation process in order to appropriate the returns of their investment (Dahlander and Wallin, 2006). Owners of open source projects typically have several options to open up or restrict access to the software and the development process. Shah (2006) coined the term "gated communities". It implies that the project initiator controls the permeability of the community, e.g. by imposing restrictive property rights of the software or by excluding non-corporate members from code integration and decision-making. As Shah noted, value appropriation may sometimes negatively affect value creation by the community. She observed that contributions were low in a tightly controlled environment like the gated community but participation was lively in a broadly accessible open source project governed by a heterogeneous community. Also West and O'Mahony (2008) indicated in their analysis of sponsored open source communities that firms managing an open source project need to balance the level of control and opportunities for outside contributors in order to create a sustainable participation architecture. Dahlander and Magnusson (2005) explained why this balancing act of managing a community is a key issue: With too much control communities may not contribute with all of their energy, interest, and creativity. With too little control the results may not serve the firm's goals. Therefore they suggest that firms should seek a symbiotic relationship with their communities in order to stimulate contributions while retaining control by subtle means. Interaction between voluntary communities and software firms have allowed O'Mahony and Bechky (2008) to observe the conciliation of divergent interests through collaboration in non-profit foundations. Still, only few research has quantitatively explored the impact of firm control on communities. As one of the dissertation papers has found (von Krogh et al., 2009a), transparency of the project's management and the reputation of the firm positively influence contributors' efforts. Accessibility for the open source community, however, has only a weakly positive impact.

2.3. Competitive Dynamics

Thirdly, analyzing open source projects raises an intriguing question on competitive dynamics: Why do firms give away for free valuable investments in the form of source code? The fact that this happens implies that firms benefit in a certain way when they freely reveal some of their technologies. Already in the beginning of the nineties Garud and Kumaraswamy (1993) noted the success of Sun Microsystem's knowledge revealing strategy by being the first to break proprietary barriers. On the one hand the company benefited from network externalities of its products which diffused at a higher rate than their competitor's solutions. On the other hand sponsoring open technologies allowed Sun to be the first to implement it in new products thus gaining temporal competitive advantage. From an economic point of view, free revealing of innovations benefits firms in various ways, among others through reputation gain (Harhoff et al., 2003) and better opportunities for R&D partnerships (Muller and Pénin, 2005) as well as increased technology diffusion (Pénin, 2007) and standard setting (Bonaccorsi and Rossi, 2003; West and Gallagher, 2006). A common value appropriation strategy for open source software involves selective revealing of knowledge. Henkel (2006) found in his study on embedded Linux firms that they revealed about half of their code while protecting the other half. Such selective revealing strategies have been common practice in the IT industry as cases of Apple and Sun Microsystems showed (West, 2003). In one of the dissertation papers the case of Nokia is elaborated where partial revealing of knowledge also plays a key role (Stuermer et al., 2009).

Intuitively, imitation by competitors may appear to be a great threat for firms investing in open source projects. However, the mere use of open source software does not destroy the firm's competitive advantage since the open source license of the technology already has turned it into a commodity (West, 2003). It is the creation and maintenance of a symbiotic community which may become the source of sustainable competitive advantage (Dahlander and Magnusson, 2008). The capability to manage an external community enables a firm to access its knowledge and quickly integrate it into new products. By extending this core idea of open innovation (Chesbrough, 2003), one of the dissertation papers explains how IBM was able to create and maintain a broad community for its open source project Eclipse (Spaeth et al., 2009a). Already during the first years after the release of the platform, programmers not employed by IBM started offering contributions. The external community has been growing continuously ever since, forming about half of the Eclipse developers' population in 2007, the time of the study. This example shows that investing in open source projects and building an active community can create a valuable resource difficult to imitate by competitors. Von Krogh (2002) has defined communities as resources of firms but has also pointed out the dilemma that once a community displays a high level of voluntary action and self-organization, the ability to control it from the outside decreases.

2.4. Characterizing Firm-Sponsored Open Source Projects

The previous sections distinguish between two types of open source projects: community-driven and firm-managed initiatives. Although this distinction has been made before in the research on open source communities by West and O'Mahony (2005 and 2008), the definition of a firm-sponsored open source project has remained vague or too simplified. A more precise description is necessary because several dimensions have to be taken into account in order to position a community. O'Mahony (2007) lists five principles of a community-managed open source project which determine its governance structure: independence, pluralism, permeable representation, decentralized decision-making, and autonomous participation. Therefore, a firm-driven open source project may be defined by the opposite of these characteristics: dependence on a single sponsor, dominance of one company, undisputed control by one sponsor, centralized decision-making by the company's management, and strictly restricted participation.

While both extreme types of communities do exist in the open source universe, many intermediary forms prevail. As has happened in the subsequently described case of Eclipse, the initiating firm may for example relinquish control by creating an independent foundation and assigning it with the leadership of the open source project. Or decision-making can be substantially influenced by the will of the community as was the case with the Openmoko project. This shows that although a firm-initiated open source project usually starts off at the extreme position, it may shift towards a more accessible, community-managed structure if the company allows it to.

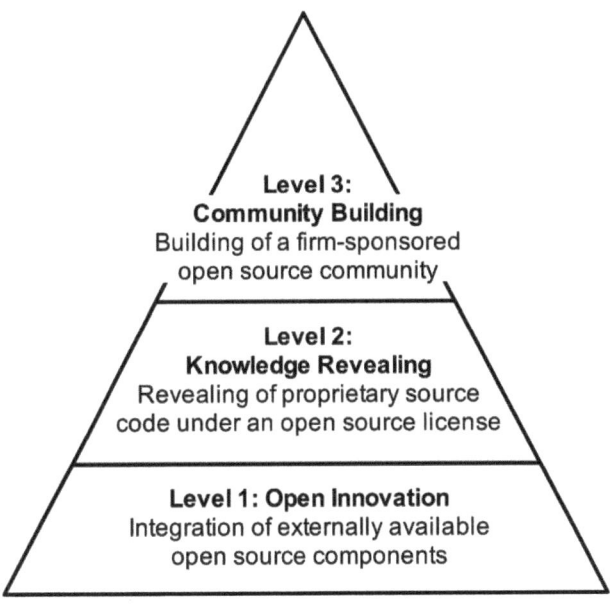

Figure 1: Adoption levels of the open source development model

In this context O'Mahony (2007) has introduced the concept of *primarily independent elements* of the open source development model. According to this analysis firms can determine their adoption level of the open source model by choosing their position on one of three basic levels (see Figure 1): The first level involves integration of externally available knowledge which is better known as 'open innovation' in the sense of Chesbrough (2003). Alternatively, a company directing an open source project can employ legal elements by freely revealing source code under an open source license (von Hippel and von Krogh, 2006). The control of the development process, however, remains fully governed by the firm. Finally, to apply the community element, too, the firm has to renounce some of the project's governance in order to create a prospering community (Shah, 2006).

Usually companies are free to choose up to which level they want to adopt the open source development model. While some firms such as Motorola have decided to use open source components without deliberately revealing own developments nor intending to attract outside contributors, other companies such as Nokia or IBM have chosen to publish open source code and also build an external developer community (Stuermer et al., 2009; Spaeth et al., 2009a). Why did they reveal more knowledge than they were obliged to by the software license? The model of private-collective innovation provides an explanation.

2.5. The Private-Collective Model of Innovation

The private-collective model of innovation represents a combination of the private investment model and the collective-action innovation model (von Hippel and von Krogh, 2003). In the private investment model innovators appropriate financial returns from innovations through intellectual property rights such as patents, copyright, licenses, or trade secrets within the legal framework imposed by society. Any knowledge spillover will reduce the innovator's benefits. Thus freely revealed knowledge is not in the interest of the innovator.

The collective-action innovation model explains the creation of public goods which are defined by the non-rivalry of benefits and non-excludable access to the good. In this case the innovators do not benefit more than anyone else not investing into the public good, thus free-riding may occur. In response to this problem, the cost of innovation has to be distributed. Therefore governments typically invest into public goods through public funding.

Combining these two concepts the private-collective model of innovation explains the creation of *public* goods through *private* funding. The model is based on the assumption that an innovator privately creating a public good will benefit more than a free-rider just consuming the public good. While the result of the investment is equally available to both, the innovator benefits from the very process of creating the public good (Spaeth et al., 2008). In the case of open source software production, the programming code as explicit knowledge is freely revealed and accessible to all, even to competitors. Nonetheless, the innovator gains tacit knowledge and expertise through the creation process representing an advantage which is difficult to imitate (Grand et al., 2004). Therefore, private-collective innovation occurs on a sustainable basis when the process-related rewards exceed the process-related costs (von Krogh, 2008).

Typical benefits of firms investing in public goods have been analyzed in open source development (von Hippel and von Krogh, 2006). These benefits include low knowledge protection costs, learning effects for the firm, reputation gain, high diffusion level of innovations, creation of external innovations, lower manufacturing costs, and faster time-to-market (Stuermer et al., 2009). However, as the case study on Nokia shows private-collective innovation activities also involve costs such as loss of differentiation from competitors, leakage of business secrets, investments into community creation and maintenance, loss of control, and efficiency loss caused by organizational changes.

3. Research Framework

This dissertation seeks to shed light on two issues related to community building and firm-sponsored open source projects. First, what are the main benefits and costs for firms conducting private-collective innovation by investing in open source projects? And second, since the collaboration of firms with external communities affects their incentive structures, how are the contributions influenced by the involvement of commercially oriented technology companies? These questions point to gaps in the literature where previous research has not yet found answers.

3.1. Filling Gaps in the Literature

In earlier studies economists have conceptualized possible benefits derived from knowledge revealing by firms (Harhoff, 1996; Harhoff et al., 2003; Muller and Pénin, 2005; Pénin, 2007). Analyzing the options and consequences of a firm's openness in its research and development activities has provided interesting theoretical insights. However, while the models promise attractive returns from investments in publicly available knowledge resources, the applicability of the theory has yet to be proved.

By reviewing empirical research in various industries and analyzing the case of the open source development model in depth, von Hippel and von Krogh (2006) have found that firms in the past have abandoned monopoly positions by disclosing innovations. This unintuitive behavior was explained by the underlying benefits firms gain during the knowledge revealing process. Yet, while the conceptual study perfectly integrates the models of private-collective innovations, no new evidence is presented in order to prove the validity of the arguments.

Therefore, this dissertation presents three pivotal studies which empirically analyze the benefit and cost structure of private-collective innovation and find options for organizational interventions in order to increase the contributions of external communities. The strength of these independent research projects lies in the diverse selection of methods (longitudinal data, grounded theory building, and structured equation modeling) and dataset (quantitative archival data, expert interviews, and online survey) providing a holistic view on firm-sponsored open source projects. Each study uses a unique set of data and applies a different method of analysis as will be described subsequently.

3.2. Extending the Open Innovation Paradigm

The first paper "Enabling Knowledge Creation through Outsiders: Towards a Push Model of Open Innovation" (Spaeth et al., 2009a) presents a perspective on the deficiencies of the current concept of open innovation in explaining external knowledge creation. Chesbrough (2003) defines open innovation as adding external knowledge to internal research and development processes and selling unused internal innovations on external markets. However, this does not explain why and how the outside knowledge was produced in the first place. The extended model of open innovation therefore attempts to describe how firms may facilitate the creation of product-related knowledge receiving it 'pushed-back' into its internal innovation processes instead of having to 'pull-back' this knowledge themselves.

The study illustrates IBM's creation of and continued investments in the open source platform Eclipse. Based on quantitative archival data of communication and production processes and comparing the contributions of IBM versus non-

IBM individuals, the ratio of knowledge revealing versus knowledge reception is calculated. The longitudinal analysis shows that during a six year period around 70 IBM-employed developers were constantly programming for Eclipse. While in the beginning external participation was low, it increased up to a 100 active contributors after IBM gave up much of its control of the open source project. Details on the case are elaborated in the next section.

3.3. Nokia's Entrance Into the Open Source Industry

The second paper "Extending private-collective innovation: a case study" (Stuermer et al., 2009) conducts an in-depth qualitative analysis of a corporate-sponsored open source project. The case of Nokia's mobile device platform Maemo represents a successful new product development process based on an open source technology stack. Through integration of external innovations Nokia was able to create a new mobile device very quickly. To this end, Nokia invested into the building of a user and developer community. These and other activities of private-collective innovation created costs unrecognized until then. Therefore, the paper presents an analysis of benefits and costs of this distributed type of innovation.

To provide an empirical basis 23 in-depth expert interviews with Nokia managers and engineers, contractors, and voluntary community members were conducted leading to around 250 pages of transcripts. The semi-structured interview guideline was designed to find causal relationships between the firm's activities and their consequences. The questions treated issues like e.g. knowledge revealing strategies, community activity, and organizational issues such as recruiting or forms of collaborations. With the support of a computer-aided qualitative data analysis software the transcribed interviews were consolidated into 12 constructs following the grounded theory building method (Glaser and Strauss, 1967).

3.4. Antecedents of Intrinsic and Extrinsic Motivation

The third paper "The credible sponsor: Participants' motivation and organization attributes in collaborative digital innovation" looks at the sponsoring effect on the contributers' motivation and on their performance. While previous studies have concentrated on the causes of motivation within community-managed open source projects (Hertel et al., 2003; Stewart and Gosain, 2006; Roberts et al., 2006), this research project analyzes the effect of perceived firm characteristics on the intrinsic and extrinsic motivation of voluntary contributors.

In order to assess the significance and impact of the attributes of firm perception (knowledge revealing, accessibility, and corporate credibility), a survey was sent to the two independent communities of Maemo and Openmoko. Within two weeks 1233 individuals filled out the questionnaire corresponding to a response rate of 27.9 percent. The items were grouped into constructs and then analyzed by a structured equation model. The results show that the firm's credibility has the highest impact on the intrinsic motivation of contributors while knowledge revealing and accessibility were significant only on a low impact level. Counterintuitively the model shows extrinsic motivation to exert a slightly higher positive effect on contribution level than intrinsic motivation.

4. Three Cases of Firm-Sponsored Open Source Communities

In the following section the three firm-sponsored open source communities will be characterized. They were analyzed qualitatively and quantitatively in the dissertation papers in the references representing the empirical evidence of this thesis. In the following case summaries emphasis is placed on relevant interdependencies between individuals, communities, other stakeholders, and the firm which initiated the open source project. Insight shall be gained in the different reasons of technology companies to found and continuously sponsor their own open source project and how they manage issues such as governance, control and motivation of developers. First, the case of Eclipse, the software development environment founded by IBM, is portrayed. Next, Nokia's open source community Maemo is described. Finally, the history and background of the mobile phone project Openmoko is presented.

4.1. Eclipse by IBM

On February 22, 1996 IBM announced the acquisition of Object Technology International Inc. (OTI), a leading development firm of object-oriented software technology (Business Wire, 1996). OTI remained an autonomous subsidiary of IBM Canada employing about 100 highly skilled developers (O'Mahony et al., 2005). At that time IBM was looking for a common technology platform to unite their various software solutions using Java as a programming language. The OTI team was appointed to develop this key platform for IBM and other corporate partners so they could create complementary products with it. In 2000 the platform was named 'Eclipse' and gained internal adoption throughout IBM. Since IBM's strategy was to make money not from client or development software but from server software (e.g. WebSphere), they decided to release Eclipse as open source software in order to gain the maximum market share in software development tools (West, 2003). With this move they convinced partner firms to use and extend Eclipse because they did not have to fear to be locked into a proprietary platform.

The management of IBM was aware that starting an open source project involved more than publishing the source code on some website. According to O'Mahony and colleagues (2005) the Eclipse team adapted its processes and practiced for several months to collaborate in an open source development mode e.g. by setting up mailing lists and newsgroups and communicating internally in a transparent way. The Eclipse managers also wanted to attract corporate partners. Thus they invited other software firms to join the board of stewards governing the future direction of the open source project. The members were granted equal decision rights in the consortium but IBM remained the legal owner of Eclipse.

In November 2001 the public responded positively to the announcement of IBM releasing its 40 million dollar investment Eclipse as an open source project (see e.g. commentary by Gartner analysts Feiman and Driver, 2001). During the following months many more companies joined the consortium and started building extensions for the platform. Eclipse evolved as a typical sponsor-driven open source project including public source code and public mailing lists. However, the effective role of IBM remained unclear because consortium members as well as the public perceived Eclipse as still mainly controlled by IBM.

In conversation with the consortium members the IBM management proposed a new governance model based on the structures of successful community-managed open source organizations such as the Apache Foundation. In February

2004 the new non-profit Eclipse Foundation was created owning the intellectual property rights of the software platform, taking care of the technical infrastructure, managing the release process, and undertaking public relations and marketing activities. Simultaneously the foundation demanded more formal commitment from its members including up to 500'000 dollar annual membership fee and employment of several full-time Eclipse developers.

The strategic move by IBM to give up its privileged role as owner of Eclipse and to create an independent foundation proved successful. Many more large corporations joined the Eclipse Foundation since its start (e.g. HP, Intel, Nokia, Motorola, Oracle, and SAP), and contributions from non-IBM developers increased substantially since 2004 representing about half of the programmer population in 2007 (Spaeth et al., 2009a).

4.2. Maemo by Nokia

Already in the year 2000 Nokia had started to experiment with the Linux kernel and other open source software (Stuermer et al., 2009). Engineers tested embedded Linux on mobile devices in Nokia's laboratory until they felt that this operating system was mature enough to be used on portable products. At the same time and totally independently, another stream of research was developing the novel product category of Internet tablets. The basic idea was to provide customers with a convenient device to browse the web, receive emails and communicate via chat and voice-over-IP. Nokia decided to use Linux as a platform for this innovative product because the software provided high flexibility and independence from other firms in order to explore the yet unknown consumer requirements of the new device category.

Inspired by this vision, Nokia designed an overall software architecture of the operating system Maemo based on open source components. Partly the engineers adapted these software components themselves and partly they contracted external open source developers for specific implementation tasks. After having signed non-disclosure agreements these programmers were assigned to adapt existing open source components to the hardware requirements of the mobile device. Through the strategy of hiring core developers well acquainted with open source technologies and development processes Nokia gained indirect access to existing open source communities.

Collaboration with and active participation in incumbent open source communities was a major process goal since the beginning of the project. Nokia deliberately chose open source components not only due to their functionality, but also based on their licensing opportunities and their community structure. The legal requirements of the open source software allowed Nokia to mix it with proprietary elements. As a goal the project's community had to be lively and diverse without the dominance of a single company (Jaaksi, 2007). Another goal was to establish an own open source community around the Maemo operating system. Nokia created a community platform for communication and collaboration. Later community building activities included e.g. a logo competition for the Maemo brand or the organization of a developers' conference. As of June 2009, there are over 18'000 registered users on the community platform sharing 861 applications for the Maemo system.

The first version of the device, the 770 Internet Tablet, was announced in May 2005. Simultaneously Nokia started its developers' device program giving away 500 products at a low price to qualified open source developers. In this way

Nokia gained rapid acceptance from skilled programmers because they enthusiastically started to develop new applications and port existing Linux programs for the Internet Tablet. Attracting these technology leaders enabled Nokia also to test the device and receive valuable feedback and even bug fixes from the community. Eventually in November 2005 the public sales of the Internet Tablet began.

While building the device using open source components and releasing source code under open source licenses, Nokia deliberately kept certain parts of the device closed as proprietary software. On the one hand they were not able to publish proprietary third-party software such as hardware drivers or the Internet browser Opera, on the other hand they retained some of their own developments such as the graphical user interface in order to prevent competitors to copy Nokia's end user experience. In addition to this, Nokia preserved complete control over the development process of the Maemo software release. Therefore, the process of development was more or less transparent while the direct influence on the feature set or timing was strictly controlled by the Nokia management.

However, Nokia granted access to software functionality and project governance by other means. Technology-wise, Nokia invested substantial effort in the provision of a free software development kit allowing skilled programmers to create applications as well as improvements at the operating system level. In this way community members were able to enhance Maemo according to their needs and without depending on Nokia's permission. And in order to permit external contributors to voice their positions more clearly, Nokia invited them to elect the Maemo Community Council in 2008. This group of five volunteers represents the community to the company. While this council has no formal authority towards Nokia it allows better communication of the interests of the community.

4.3. Openmoko by Openmoko Inc.

In 2005 the Taiwanese computer and components manufacturer First International Computer, Inc. (FIC) intended to create a smart phone based on the Windows Mobile operating system (von Krogh et al., 2009a). However, due to the project leader's lobbying the management of FIC became convinced to try a completely new way of developing a mobile phone. In order to differentiate from established smart phone manufacturers using software from third-party vendors, FIC decided to invest into the development of a completely open platform based on the Debian GNU/Linux operating system and other open source components. Although embedded Linux software manufacturers such as MontaVista existed, FIC thought they were not collaborating sufficiently with the open source community and thus not using the full potential of its innovative capabilities.

Nevertheless, revealing substantial investments of the new platform worried the management. By accessing the full software stack on a source code basis potential competitors were thought to be able to imitate FIC's product development quickly. On the other hand implementing the software with the hardware was known to be very difficult requiring know-how and experience with the platform. Therefore the project leader argued FIC would retain competitive advantage possessing the knowledge and resources to integrate the software and manufacture the devices for the mass market.

In fact, the market response was overwhelming: Soon after the product announcement in November 2006 and the beginning of the sales in July 2007, volunteer programmers and other companies started to improve FIC's platform, eventually developing different types of operating systems for the mobile phone. Analysts as well as open source developers were enthusiastic that a hardware manufacturer had finally announced the production of a completely open mobile phone.

Similar to Eclipse and Maemo, the Openmoko community, too, received an online collaboration platform in order to exchange knowledge and source code. Unique to the Openmoko management was that they not only let the outside community participate in the software development, but also involved them in the hardware selection process. For instance when the Openmoko engineers were looking for an appropriate Wi-Fi chip for the smart phone, they asked on the public mailing list if someone could recommend a certain manufacturer. Indeed, as many of the subscribers on this list were working in relevant companies, the feedback to the request was high and eventually led to the discovery of the best-suited chip set. Recently, in May 2009, Openmoko management released even the exact hardware specifications including architecture files with the computer-aided designs. With this step the company wants to test the ability of the community to contribute also to the hardware design.

Unfortunately, the Openmoko project was not so much a success from a business point of view. Although FIC decided in 2006 to spin-off the Openmoko project as an independent company and found Openmoko, Inc., recently the product planning for 2010 had to be radically changed. Partly because of the world economic crisis starting in late 2008, partly because of technical problems, the sales figures of the mobile devices did not turn out as well as expected. Thus, in February 2009 Openmoko, Inc. announced that the development of the third generation of the free mobile phone had to be postponed indefinitely while the company had started a client project in order to increase cash flow immediately. Therefore, at the time of writing, the commercial future of Openmoko is unclear.

5. Conclusions and Implications

So far, previous literature on corporate-sponsored open source communities has been reviewed and the empirical findings of this thesis have been presented. This final section completes the picture with a broader concept that characterizes the unique qualities of such a firm-influenced network of open source software producers. It is proposed to see corporate-sponsored communities as a successful example of how a firm may gain interorganizational competitive advantage through its community.

By portraying Eclipse, Maemo, and Openmoko, three cases of corporate-driven open source initiatives are presented in detail. They illustrate the statement by O'Mahony (2007) that individuals are no longer the only parties founding open source projects. In all of the above examples, large technology corporations started their own branded open source project with the goal of releasing source code in order to attract external actors to contribute to the future development effort. While the specific strategies and processes differed, all of the firms attempted not only to integrate code and reveal software, but also to actively build a symbiotic community of third-party participants (Dahlander and Magnusson, 2005). The firms made use of all three elements of the open source development model: integration of innovations, revealing of knowledge, and creation of a community (O'Mahony, 2007). The firms applied the principle of private-collective innovation and enhanced the model by creating an external community of volunteers and partner firms.

In fact, empirical evidence in the dissertation papers shows that only by building a prospering community will the benefits of private-collective innovation become fully accessible. For instance in the Maemo case reputation gain was possible only because Nokia successfully managed to start and maintain a community of volunteers and partnering firms (Stuermer et al., 2009). In the case of Eclipse the community contributed innovations only because IBM gave up control of the open source project and empowered the members of the Eclipse Foundation (Spaeth et al., 2009a). As the third dissertation study shows, the perception of the project-sponsor positively affects the behavior of the community (von Krogh et al., 2009a). The three organizational attributes knowledge revealing, accessibility, and credibility positively influence the motivation and thus the contribution level of the outside participants.

Therefore it proves necessary for firms to attract active contributors in order to benefit the most from their investments in open source technologies. Such a thriving community cannot be acquired on the market but it requires substantial, credible, and long-term commitment by the sponsor (Dahlander and Wallin, 2006). In return, such a realm of friends is not easily imitated making it a valuable asset of the firm.

5.1. The Concept of Interorganizational Competitive Advantage: Towards a Related Research Agenda

Drawing from literature, Dyer and Singh (1998) have introduced the concept of interorganizational competitive advantage. This so-called relational view constitutes an alternative to the industry structure view (Porter, 1980) and the resource-based view (Wernerfelt, 1984; Barney, 1991). According to this concept unique resources and industry position are not the exclusive requirements for gaining above-average rents. Firms may also achieve competitive advantage through a network of relationships with other organizations. Such embedded interfirm resources and routines are difficult to imitate because they require durable collaboration and cannot be acquired on the market. However, unlike resources owned by a firm alone these relationships depend on mutual understanding and trust of the partners and thus cannot be fully controlled by a single organization.

Reflecting on the qualities of firm-sponsored open source communities it becomes obvious that they represent an example of such interfirm relations. In all the cases presented the focal firms IBM, Nokia, as well as Openmoko Inc. are connected to external individuals and organizations creating a network of durable relationships. Although each company cannot completely control its partners, it is able to benefit substantially from the community it has initiated giving it an interorganizational competitive advantage as described by Dyer and Singh (1998). Analysis of their list of determinants shows that the characteristics of firm-sponsored open source communities indeed matches the definition of interorganizational competitive advantage (Table 1). In the following, *characteristics and sub-determinants of firm-sponsored open source communities* are described based on the framework of relational rents by Dyer and Singh (1998:663; the terminology of the titles in boldface is quoted from their illustration):

Determinants of relational rents	Subprocesses facilitating relational rents
1. Relation-specific assets In firm-driven open source communities: A firm creates open source software components and other artifacts collaboratively with its community.	a) **Duration of safeguards** In firm-driven open source communities: Open source software licenses protect jointly produced open source software code thus ensuring availability of the code for all at all times. b) **Volume of interfirm transactions** In firm-driven open source communities: Collaborative software development platforms on the Internet facilitate communication of the firm with its community members.
2. Knowledge-sharing routines In firm-driven open source communities: Continuous interaction between employees of the company with external community participants externalizes the firm's tacit knowledge.	a) **Partner-specific absorptive capacity** In firm-driven open source communities: Overlapping bases of the firm's and community's knowledge evolve over time e.g. when external participants read source code or manuals. b) **Incentives to encourage transparency and discourage free riding** In firm-driven open source communities: Shared norms and values by the firm and its community are critical elements favoring open communication and transparent decision processes.

3. Complementary resources and capabilities In firm-driven open source communities: Stakeholders collectively develop software such as the Linux kernel or the Eclipse platform by contributing complementary capabilities.	a) **Ability to identify and evaluate potential complementarities** In firm-driven open source communities: Through the transparent development process of open source software complementary capabilities become assessable. b) **Role of organizational complementarities to access benefits of strategic resource complementarity** In firm-driven open source communities: Collaboration of the firm with its community aligns their communication and culture over time.
4. Effective governance In firm-driven open source communities: Adaptive governance mechanisms ranging from informal agreements up to legally binding contracts enable effective collaboration between the firm and its community.	a) **Ability to employ self-enforcement rather than third-party governance enforcement** In firm-driven open source communities: As the private-collective model of innovation explains firms often contribute more to open source projects than they are legally obliged to because of process-related benefits. b) **Ability to employ informal versus formal self-enforcement governance mechanisms** In firm-driven open source communities: Firms are very much interested to act as credible members of the community in order to attract contributions from external participants.

Table 1: Firm-driven open source communities as an example of interorganizational competitive advantage (table based on Figure 1 by Dyer and Singh, 1998:663)

1. **Relation-specific assets:** As firms must do something special to develop a competitive advantage, the creation of assets has to be unique to the partners. In the case of firm-sponsored communities e.g. Nokia has collaborated closely with professional developers and open source firms specialized in certain open source components in order to assemble the integrated software platform. Such product development processes require intense knowledge exchange and transaction-specific know-how. Thus all stakeholders made substantial nonrecoverable investments for the asset by e.g. learning a certain software code and architecture. While a decade ago physical proximity was essential for interorganizational cooperation, today it is superseded by the virtual proximity derived from the Internet.

   a) **Duration of safeguards:** In order to protect their investments, the partners seek to safeguard against opportunistic behavior. In the case of open source communities it is the software license which ensures that the asset, the source code, remains equally available for all at all times (Stewart et al., 2006; Osterloh and Rota, 2007).

   b) **Volume of interfirm transactions:** Alliance partners increase their collaborative efficiency by raising the frequency and scope of transactions. In the case of corporate-sponsored open source communities this is achieved by the firms facilitating communication and contributions from within the open source community by introducing a collaborative software platform.

2. **Knowledge-sharing routines:** Interorganizational learning is argued to be critical for competitive success. In open source projects this corresponds to

intense knowledge sharing between organizations and individuals. It is facilitated by various mechanisms. On a technical side there exists a tradition of using newsgroup channels, mailing lists, wikis, forums, film clips, chat rooms and many other communication media in order to broadcast knowledge initially residing in one firm. Its diffusion outside the firm boundaries may then trigger innovations from the community and thus contribute to the development process of the software. Through continuous interaction even tacit knowledge residing within the community may be externalized as explicit knowledge (Nonaka, 1994) becoming available for use by the sponsoring firm. For instance experimentation by some community members lead to radical innovations in the case of the Maemo platform.

a) **Partner-specific absorptive capacity:** Recipients have to be able to recognize and assimilate valuable knowledge from the sender. Cohen and Levinthal (1990) therefore coined the concept of absorptive capacity. In open source communities the required overlapping knowledge bases evolve over time through frequent and often informal interactions. This enables the external community to absorb the knowledge revealed by the firm e.g. by studying the source code or reading manuals.

b) **Incentives to encourage transparency and discourage free riding:** Knowledge sharing activities are fragile and in their essence cannot be fully controlled. Therefore, appropriate incentives as well as norms are necessary to achieve a culture of sustainable knowledge exchange. As the presented cases and other research on open source communities has shown (Shah, 2006; Stewart and Gosain, 2006), norms and values are critical elements of the ideology in open source communities encouraging transparency and discouraging free riding.

3. **Complementary resources and capabilities:** Firms benefit in an alliance when they own complementary resources. In this way the collective effect is enhanced resulting in greater rents than the assets of each individual partner. Companies that are not part of the network are thus underprivileged. In the software industry examples of such synergies are found as network externalities when companies use and create compatible technologies. When firms pool their resources and collectively develop a platform such as Linux, they benefit from collective rents (West and Gallagher, 2006). Standardized components and file formats diffuse more rapidly if they are open and freely accessible (Garud and Kumaraswamy, 1993). On an organizational level foundations of open source projects (e.g. Eclipse) represent formal networks where members share benefits and costs of product development.

   a) **Ability to identify and evaluate potential complementarities:** Finding the right alliance and integrating into it successfully is a delicate endeavor. Firms have to invest substantial resources in order to identify matching partners. Transparency and permeability of open source projects enable gradual acquaintance between potential partner firms and future employees reducing the risk of a failed choice. E.g. Nokia used its firm-sponsored open source community to spot the most skilled, innovative, and motivated individuals. Through their prior participation in the community they felt attached to Nokia and were very likely to accept its recruitment offer.

b) **Role of organizational complementarities to access benefits of strategic resource complementarity:** Next to the strategic fit the organizational complementarity represents a challenge in forming alliances, too. Intense collaboration within open source communities facilitates alignment of communication and culture and therefore increases the probability of success. E.g. a common norm is reciprocity or the culture of gifts which characterizes open source communities strongly (Bergquist and Ljungberg, 2001; Lakhani and von Hippel, 2003).

4. **Effective governance:** When organizations are interconnected, it is critical in which way they behave towards each other bringing up the question of governance. Dyer and Singh distinguish between third-party enforcement of agreements (e.g. legal contracts) and self-enforcing agreements (e.g. strategic alliances). The latter is further divided between formal (e.g. financial investments) and informal (e.g. trust and reputation) safeguards (1998: 669). The authors propose that transactions should be appropriately aligned with the specific governance structures minimizing transaction costs and maximizing value creation. Looking at the governance mechanisms present in open source communities different forms of control are indeed in use, sometimes several of them in the same open source project at once. For instance in Eclipse there exist formal contracts obliging foundation members to pay certain fees and ordering engineers to program using the publicly available software code. Simultaneously, a second governance structure regulates the development process in a rather self-enforcing way by allowing participants to influence the platform's properties through their contributions.

a) **Ability to employ self-enforcement rather than third-party enforcement governance mechanisms:** According to various research self-governed mechanisms are more effective than is third-party enforcement. They save contracting, recontracting and monitoring costs, prove to be more flexible, and are more probable to induce value-creating initiatives. In addition self-enforced relationships are more difficult to copy than contractual agreements. Thus they are more likely to represent a sustainable advantage. The concept of private-collective innovation depicts an example of such a self-enforced safeguard. As described previously the model stimulates (but does not force) firms to contribute to the creation of open source software rather than just using it as free-rider.

b) **Ability to employ informal versus formal self-enforcement governance mechanisms:** Informal safeguards such as trust or reputation are much more difficult to copy than formal mechanisms like symmetric investments. While the latter can be imitated by competitors, informal safeguards require time and trustful behavior to develop. Similarly, credibility of firms within an open source community proves to be an important antecedent of intrinsic motivation leading to the conclusion that trust and reputation increase the benefits of firm-sponsored communities.

As these theoretical and empirical characteristics of interorganizational relationships have illustrated, a network of partners may result in a source of sustained competitive advantage. However, managers of such firm-sponsored communities have to bear in mind that the rents are jointly generated and owned by both sides, the corporation and the external community. The competitive advantage is extinguished either if the firm withdraws its resources from the community or if the community decides to separate itself by forking the software code (Kogut and Metiu, 2001). Therefore, wise management techniques are required by the sponsor in order to sustain a prospering community of skilled contributors and thus benefit from its competitive advantage.

5.2. Impact on Theory and Practice

On a theoretical level this dissertation contributes to the understanding of distributed innovation. On the one hand it shows that today's concept of open innovation (Chesbrough, 2003; Chesbrough and Crowther, 2006) covers only part of the reality at least within the software industry. The examples given show that firms have done far more than just integrating external innovations. Rather they have substantially released knowledge and invested in its diffusion by creating communities of volunteers and professionals. On the other hand this dissertation extends the model of private-collective innovation (von Hippel and von Krogh, 2003) by emphasizing the crucial role of value appropriation by community building. Investing into the production of public goods without actively creating relationships with other contributors would not make full use of private-collective innovation. Also, as described in the previous section, firm-managed communities are shown to represent an empirical example of the relational view as defined by Dyer and Singh (1998) illustrating comprehensively how interorganizational competitive advantage results from the relationship between the sponsoring firm and its community.

Furthermore communities in private-collective innovation represent in themselves a new form of distributed innovation. In the literature on collective innovation various concepts have evolved. Two of them shall be briefly highlighted and delineated against communities of private-collective innovation. Eric von Hippel (1986) coined the idea of lead user communities pointing out that users of technologies often achieve product innovations when they try to solve their personal problems. Such product improvements in turn can be commercialized by firms manufacturing them through mass production. While the concept of user innovation is often taken as theoretical explanation for open source communities (von Hippel, 2001), it does not take into account that in firm-sponsored projects the community building activity is started by a firm, not by the user. Therefore communities in private-collective innovation are a separate concept of collective innovation because they follow a different path of initiation.

Another concept are communities of practice (Brown and Duguid, 1991; Wenger and Snyder, 2000). These groups of professionals with similar interests inside an organization meet to find novel solutions for problems and thereby help to drive strategy, start new lines of businesses, transfer best practices, develop skills, and recruit and retain talent. Communities in private-collective innovation differ from communities of practice mainly by their cross-boundary participation. Although often a majority of contributions stems from the sponsor of the community, it is the fundamental goal of communities in private-collective innovation to enable and encourage external participation.

On the practical side managers of software companies is shown the great benefits of building a community. Though just a rough estimate, the case study on Eclipse shows that external firms and individuals contributed software code valued at approximately 1.7 billion USD (Spaeth et al., 2009a). However, revealing knowledge and investing in the creation of communities also incurs costs which have to be considered in strategic decisions (Stuermer et al., 2009).

For policy makers, this dissertation shows possible economic advantage of supporting the use and development of open source software. The private-collective model of innovation illustrates how firms may be incentivized to invest in the production of public good. Therefore, establishing a stimulating environment for firms to create and integrate open source software may possibly multiply the economic benefits for society in comparison to allowing incumbent proprietary software firms to collect monopoly rents.

5.3. Future Research Agenda

Although literature on open source communities is abundant, research-wise the phenomenon is nowhere near consummated. Within the context of firm-sponsored open source communities many questions remain regarding governance. E.g. what is the optimal level of control which a firm should exert on its community? As has been shown it is a precarious balancing act: If the company loosens the reins too much, the software project may not evolve in the intended direction or competitors may imitate the technology all too quickly. If the strings are tightened too much, the credibility of the sponsor drops and motivation and performance decrease. Or even worse, the external community actively opposes the sponsoring firm and spins-off by forking the software code (Kogut and Metiu, 2001). Therefore future studies on balancing control and value appropriation of communities are of great interest to researchers as well as managers.

Focusing particularly on the forking phenomenon, a thorough empirical analysis could clarify what characteristics of control and openness have led to community splittings in the past and which factors have determined the success respectively the failure of the renegades. Research so far has mostly looked at successful communities. Analyzing the behavior of firms and individuals which have caused a forking of the project could lead to a better understanding of how to prevent this usually wearing-out process. Studying so-to-speak failed projects could also help to clarify the unique factors of successful projects leading to a clearer definition of sustainable community management.

Another strategic challenge is the decision on what kind of knowledge should be revealed and what not in order to attract external contributions. West (2003) has titled this dilemma bluntly "How open is open enough?" It represents another balancing act between revealing of knowledge and thus enabling and cultivating participation, and retaining innovations and thus being able to appropriate their value more easily. So-called selective revealing has been analyzed (Henkel, 2006), a generic theory, however, as well as practically applicable rules are still missing. Also related to this issue is the question how much of a competitive contribution can a community provide and how sustainable is it. While e.g. Openmoko Inc. successfully created a helpful community, it could not prevent the product sales from dropping. Therefore, knowing the impact of the community's innovativeness on the overall business success might help future product development investments to better appoint its resources.

Finally, finding sustainable business models of firms investing in open source technologies represents an intriguing quest for strategy researchers as well practitioners. As Dahlander and Wallin (2006) found, open source software development in its original sense is very diverse. Broadly independent communities create open source components which may even compete for being employed in end-user applications (Spaeth et al., 2009b). Therefore, firms often fill in the gap as so-called distributors integrating the components and applications as compact software solutions as in the case of Nokia and Openmoko Inc.[1] For creating the Maemo platform, Nokia for instance contracted several specialized individuals and small businesses in order to demand low-level changes on some components. Nowadays it is Nokia's strength to integrate all these interdependent parts into a complete end-consumer product. Acting as system integrator may be an attractive position in the value chain of complex technology products, as Brusoni and colleagues (2001) argued in their empirical study of the aircraft engine control system industry. Future research could advance findings of the evolution of such interconnected systems and provide advice on how to manage them efficiently (von Krogh et al., 2009b). Also qualitative and quantitative studies on firms assembling open source software are necessary to gain more insight into the classical organizational research question of differentiation and integration (Lawrence and Lorsch, 1967).

The delicate position of firms starting and managing an open source project has been illustrated. It has become apparent that only when firms sponsor open source projects in a substantial and credible way while carefully accepting the norms and rules of the external contributors, a thriving community will evolve. By analyzing and interpreting the myriad facets of communities in private-collective innovation and by providing a characterization of such communities,

---

[1] It needs to be noted that there are some successfully managed bundles of open source software packages such as the Debian GNU/Linux distribution. This is particularly important since it represents a comprehensive source for sampling open source components (Spaeth et al., 2007).

this dissertation hopes to help firms to succeed in the balancing act of entering into sustainable relationships with outside participants.

References

Alexy, O. & Leitner, M. (2008), 'Norms, Rewards, and their Effect on the Motivation of Open Source Software Developers', Technical report, Technical University of Munich.

Bae, J. & Cameron, G. T. (2006) 'Conditioning effect of prior reputation on perception of corporate giving', *Public Relations Review* **32**, 144-150.

Barney, J. (1991), 'Firm Resources And Sustained Competitive Advantage', *Journal of Management* **17**(1), 99-120.

Bergquist, M. & Ljungberg, J. (2001), 'The Power of Gifts: Organizing Social Relationships in Open Source Communities', *Information Systems Journal* **11**(4), 305-320.

Bonaccorsi, A. & Rossi, C. (2003), 'Why Open Source software can succeed', *Research Policy* **32**(7), 1243-1258.

Brown, J. S. & Duguid, P. (1991), 'Organizational Learning and Communities-of-Practice', *Organization Science* **2**, 40-57.

Brusoni, S.; Prencipe, A. & Pavitt, K. (2001), 'Knowledge Specialization, Organizational Coupling, And The Boundaries Of The Firm: Why Do Firms Know More Than They Make?', *Administrative Science Quarterly* **46**(4), 597-621.

BusinessWire (1996), 'IBM To Acquire Object Technology International Inc', http://findarticles.com/p/articles/mi_m0EIN/is_1996_Feb_22/ai_18023630, accessed June 10, 2009..

Chesbrough, H. (2003), *Open innovation. The new imperative for creating and profiting from technology*, Harvard Business School Press.

Chesbrough, H. & Crowther, A. K. (2006), 'Beyond High Tech: Early Adopters Of Open Innovation In Other Industries', *R&D Management* **36**(3), 229-236.

Cohen, W. M. & Levinthal, D. A. (1990), 'Absorptive Capacity: A New Perspective on Learning and Innovation', *Administrative Science Quarterly* **35**, 128-152.

Dahlander, L. & Magnusson, M. (2008), 'How do Firms Make Use of Open Source Communities?', *Long Range Planning* **41**(6), 629-649.

Dahlander, L. & Magnusson, M. G. (2005), 'Relationships between open source software companies and communities: Observations from Nordic firms', *Research Policy* **34**(4), 481-493.

Dahlander, L. & Wallin, M. (2006), 'A man on the inside: Unlocking communities as complementary assets', *Research Policy* **35**(8), 1243-1259.

Dyer, J. H. & Singh, H. (1998), 'The Relational View: Cooperative Strategy and Sources of Interorganizational Competitive Advantage', *Academy of Management Review* **23**(4), 660-679.

Feiman, J. & Driver, M. (2001), 'Commentary: Eclipse, a developer's dream?', http://news.cnet.com/2009-1001-275495.html, accessed June 10, 2009..

Franck, E. & Jungwirth, C. (2003), 'Reconciling Rent-Seekers and Donators – The Governance Structure of Open Source', *Journal of Management and Governance* **7**(4), 401-421.

Frey, B. S. & Jegen, R. (2001), 'Motivation Crowding Theory', *Journal of Economic Surveys* **15**(5), 589-611.

Frey, B. S. & Oberholzer-Gee, F. (1997), 'The Cost of Price Incentives: An Empirical Analysis of Motivation Crowding-Out', *American Economic Review* **87**(4), 746-755.

Glaser, B. & Strauss, A. (1967), *The discovery of grounded theory: Strategies for qualitative research*, Chicago: Aldine.

Grand, S.; von Krogh, G.; Leonard, D. & Swap, W. (2004), 'Resource Allocation Beyond Firm Boundaries: A Multi-Level Model for Open Source Innovation', *Long Range Planning* **37**, 591-610.

Grant, R. M. (1996), 'Toward a Knowledge-based Theory of the Firm', *Strategic Management Journal, Special Issue: Knowledge and the Firm* **17**, 109-122.

Harhoff, D. (1996), 'Strategic Spillovers And Incentives For Research And Development', *Management Science* **42**(6), 907-925.

Harhoff, D.; Henkel, J. & von Hippel, E. (2003), 'Profiting From Voluntary Information Spillovers: How Users Benefit By Freely Revealing Their Innovations', *Research Policy* **32**, 1753-1769.

Hars, A. & Ou, S. (2002), 'Working for free? Motivations for participating in open-source projects', *International Journal of Electronic Commerce* **6**, 25-39.

Henkel, J. (2006), 'Selective Revealing In Open Innovation Processes: The Case Of Embedded Linux', *Research Policy* **35**(7), 953-969.

Hertel, G.; Niedner, S. & Herrmann, S. (2003), 'Motivation of software developers in Open Source projects: an Internet-based survey of contributors to the Linux kernel', *Research Policy* **32**(7), 1159-1177.

von Hippel, E. (2001), 'Innovation By User Communities: Learning From Open-Source Software', *Sloan Management Review* **42**(4), 82-86.

von Hippel, E. (1986), 'Lead Users: A Source Of Novel Product Concepts', *Management Science* **32**(7), 791-805.

von Hippel, E. & von Krogh, G. (2006), 'Free revealing and the private-collective model for innovation incentives', *R&D Management* **36**(3), 295-306.

von Hippel, E. & von Krogh, G. (2003), 'Open Source Software and the "Private-Collective" Innovation Model: Issues for Organization Science', *Organization Science* **14**(2), 209-223.

Jaaksi, A. (2007), Experiences on Product Development with Open Source Software, *in* Joseph Feller; Brian Fitzgerald; Walt Scacchi & Alberto Sillitti, ed.,'Open Source Development, Adoption and Innovation', Boston: Springer, , pp. 85-96.

Kroah-Hartman, G.; Corbet, J. & McPherson, A. (2008), 'Linux Kernel Development: How Fast it is Going, Who is Doing It, What They are Doing, and Who is Sponsoring It', Technical report, The Linux Foundation.

von Krogh, G. (2008), Researching the Private-Collective Innovation Model, in Daved Barry & Hans Hansen, ed.,'The SAGE Handbook of New Approaches in Management and Organization', Sage, 396-397.

von Krogh, G. (2002), 'The Communal Resource And Information Systems', *The Journal Of Strategic Information Systems* **11**, 85-107.

von Krogh, G. & von Hippel, E. (2006), 'The Promise of Research on Open Source Software', *Management Science, Special Issue on open source software* **52**, 975-983.

von Krogh, G. & Spaeth, S. (2007), 'The open source software phenomenon: Characteristics that promote research', *The Journal of Strategic Information Systems* **16**(3), 236-253.

von Krogh, G.; Spaeth, S.; Haefliger, S. & Wallin, M. (2008), 'Open Source Software: What we know (and do not know) about motives to contribute', ETH Zurich.

von Krogh, G.; Spaeth, S.; Stuermer, M. & Hertel, G. (2009a), 'The credible sponsor: Participants' motivation and firm attributes in collaborative digital innovation', ETH Zurich.

von Krogh, G.; Stuermer, M.; Geipel, M.; Spaeth, S.; Haefliger, S. & Baldwin, C. (2009b), 'How component dependencies predict change in complex technologies', ETH Zurich and Harvard Business School.

Lakhani, K. R. & von Hippel, E. (2003), 'How open source software works: "free" user-to-user assistance', *Research Policy* **32**(6), 923-943.

Lawrence, P. R. & Lorsch, J. W. (1967), 'Differentiation and Integration in Complex Organizations', *Administrative Science Quarterly* **12**(1), 1-47.

Lee, G. K. & Cole, R. E. (2003), 'From a Firm-Based to a Community-Based Model of Knowledge Creation: The Case of the Linux Kernel Development', *Organization Science* **14**, 633-649.

Lerner, J. & Tirole, J. (2002), 'Some Simple Economics of Open Source', *Journal of Industrial Economics* **50**(2), 197-234.

Liebeskind, J. P. (1996), 'Knowledge, strategy, and the theory of the firm', *Strategic Management Journal, Special Issue: Knowledge and the Firm* **17**, 93-107.

Markus, M. L. (2007), 'The governance of free/open source software projects: monolithic, multidimensional, or configurational?', *Journal of Management and Governance* **11**(2), 151-163.

Muller, P. & Pénin, J. (2006), 'Why Do Firms Disclose Knowledge And How Does It Matter?', *Journal of Evolutionary Economics* **16**(1-2), 85-108.

Nonaka, I. (1994), 'A Dynamic Theory of Organizational Knowledge Creation', *Organization Science* **5**, 14-37.

O'Mahony, S. (2003), 'Guarding The Commons: How Community Managed Software Projects Protect Their Work', *Research Policy* **32**(7), 1179-1198.

O'Mahony, S.; Diaz, F. C. & Mamas, E. (2005), 'Harvard Business School Case Study: IBM and Eclipse (A) and (B)', Technical report, Harvard Business School Case Study.

O'Mahony, S. & Ferraro, F. (2007), 'The Emergence Of Governance In An Open Source Community', *Academy of Management Journal* **50**(5).

O'Mahony, S. (2007), 'The governance of open source initiatives: what does it mean to be community managed?', *Journal of Management and Governance* **11**(2), 139-150.

O'Mahony, S. & Bechky, B. A. (2008), 'Boundary Organizations: Enabling Collaboration among Unexpected Allies', *Administrative Science Quarterly* **53**(3 Special Issue: Social Movements in Organizations and Markets), 422-459.

Osterloh, M. & Rota, S. (2007), 'Open source software development—Just another case of collective invention?', *Research Policy* **36**(2), 157-171.

Porter, M. E. (1980), 'Competitive Strategy', *New York: Free Press*.

Pénin, J. (2007), 'Open Knowledge Disclosure: An Overview Of The Evidence And Economic Motivations', *Journal of Economic Surveys* **21**(2), 326-347.

Raymond, E. S. (1999), *The Cathedral & the Bazaar*, 1st Edition. O'Reilly, Sebastopol, CA.

Roberts, J.; Hann, H. & Slaughter, S. (2006), 'Understanding the motivations, participation, and performance of open source software developers: A longitudinal study of the Apache projects', *Management Science* **52**(7), 984-999.

Shah, S. (2006), 'Motivation, Governance, And The Viability Of Hybrid Forms In Open Source Software Development', *Management Science* **52**(7), 1000-1014.

Spaeth, S.; Haefliger, S.; von Krogh, G. & Renzl, B. (2008), 'Communal resources in open source software development', *Information Research* **13**(1).

Spaeth, S.; Stuermer, M.; Haefliger, S. & von Krogh, G. (2007), Sampling In Open Source Software Development: The Case For Using The Debian Gnu/Linux Distribution, *in* 'HICSS 2007 40th Annual Hawaii International Conference on System Sciences'.

Spaeth, S.; Stuermer, M. & von Krogh, G. (2009a), 'Enabling Knowledge Creation Through Outsiders: Towards a Push Model of Open Innovation', *International Journal of Technology Management* (Forthcoming Special Issue on Open Innovation).

Spaeth, S.; von Krogh, G.; Stuermer, M. & Haefliger, S. (2009b), 'A Lightweight Model of Component Reuse: A Study of Software Packages in Debian GNU/Linux', Technical report, ETH Zurich.

Stewart, K.; Ammeter, A. & Maruping, L. (2006), 'Impacts of License Choice and Organizational Sponsorship on User Interest and Development Activity in Open Source Software Projects', *Information Systems Research* **17**(2), 126-144.

Stewart, K. J. & Gosain, S. (2006), 'The Impact Of Ideology On Effectiveness In Open Source Software Development Teams', *MIS Quarterly* **30**(2), 291-314.

Stuermer, M. (2005), 'Open Source Community Building', Master's thesis, University of Berne.

Stuermer, M.; Spaeth, S. & von Krogh, G. (2009), 'Extending private-collective innovation: a case study', *R&D Management* **39**(2), 170-191.

Teece, D. J. (1986), 'Profiting from technological innovation: Implications for integration, collaboration, licensing and public policy', *Research Policy* **15**(6), 285-305.

Wernerfelt, B. (1984), 'A Resource-Based View of the Firm', *Strategic Management Journal* **5**, 171-180.

West, J. (2003), 'How open is open enough? Melding proprietary and open source platform strategies', *Research Policy* **32**(7), 1259-1285.

West, J. & Gallagher, S. (2006), 'Challenges of open innovation: the paradox of firm investment in open-source software', *R&D Management* **36**(3), 319-331.

West, J. & O'Mahony, S. (2008), 'The Role of Participation Architecture in Growing Sponsored Open Source Communities', *Industry & Innovation* **15**(2), 145-168.

West, J. & O'Mahony, S. (2005), 'Contrasting Community Building In Sponsored And Community Founded Open Source Projects', *Proceedings of the 38th Annual Hawai'i International Conference on System Sciences*.

Wu, C.; Gerlach, J. H. & Young, C. E. (2007), 'An Empirical Analysis of Open Source Software Developers' Motivations and Continuance Intentions', *Information and Management* **44**(3), 253-262.

Die VDM Verlagsservicegesellschaft sucht für wissenschaftliche Verlage abgeschlossene und herausragende

Dissertationen, Habilitationen, Diplomarbeiten, Master Theses, Magisterarbeiten usw.

für die kostenlose Publikation als Fachbuch.

Sie verfügen über eine Arbeit, die hohen inhaltlichen und formalen Ansprüchen genügt, und haben Interesse an einer honorarvergüteten Publikation?

Dann senden Sie bitte erste Informationen über sich und Ihre Arbeit per Email an *info@vdm-vsg.de*.

Sie erhalten kurzfristig unser Feedback!

VDM Verlagsservicegesellschaft mbH
Dudweiler Landstr. 99   Telefon +49 681 3720 174
D - 66123 Saarbrücken   Fax   +49 681 3720 1749

www.vdm-vsg.de

Die VDM Verlagsservicegesellschaft mbH vertritt

Printed by Books on Demand GmbH, Norderstedt / Germany